AND I WONDER...

AND I WONDER...

FLIGHTS OF INSPIRATION

GAIL BOENNING

Editor: Noosha Ravaghi

for creativity and the magic of storytelling

The aim of life is self-development. To realize one's nature perfectly — that is what each of us is here for.

~Oscar Wilde

CONTENTS

1

UNCOVER

There is a process
to unbundle from our winter wear
when we come in from the cold.

Remove mittens, hat, and balaclava.
Toss them in their bin by the door.

Unlace and slip out of snowy boots.
Place them on the wire shelving
under heavily laden coat hooks.

Remove the dog's leash and collar.
Loop them over the wall peg that's attached to the wall
beneath a photo of a horse named Barnaby.

Give the tail-wagger a bone to chew...
She won't move until she gets one.

Unzip and remove my coat.
Hang it on —
Wait a minute...

What's that on my mitten?

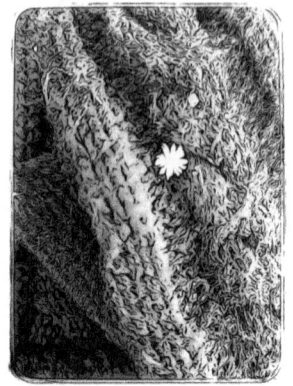

A flower remnant,
perfectly formed,
with petals 'round a button center.

And I wonder...
How much do I miss
while working my routines?

2

TEACH

Three happy puppies
wag their tails.

The first black Lab…

Elsa nudges my hand with her snout.
A tennis ball rests at my feet.
Throw it! Throw it!
Again! I insist!
Throooooooow it!

She is large in stature and personality.
As a puppy, she eats wood window sills.
She stays just out of reach
when it is time to hop in the car
to go home from the field of play,
and she plucks her own tomato and green pepper snacks
from our garden.

As an adult,
she sneaks away from home

to raid the neighbors trash cans,
stoically endures chemotherapy and surgeries to treat cancer,
and welcomes our human baby boy
with a heart of gold.

Joy-filled stories...
Frustrating stories...
Sad stories...
Living stories...
Elsa teaches me what I need to learn
so that I can keep going.

Dog #1 teaches me how to truly care for another living being.

The second black Lab...

The human baby,
now aged six years,
holds puppy Mara
against his camouflage sweatshirt.

Timid,
she refuses the first meal we offer her
in her new home.
She always stays close,
never tries to leave the yard unattended,
and loves to snuggle.

Too clever for her own good,
she outwits the cabinet safety lock
to steal chicken bones from the trash can.
For much of her life
she's troubled by a mysterious mouth infection
that leaves her near toothless
when her time comes to leave this world.

When she looks at me,
I'm certain that I am her *one*
and for many days after she dies,
sobs of grief rock me to my core.

Laugh out loud stories...
Feel warm and fuzzy stories...
Ouch stories...
Living stories...
Mara teaches me what I need to learn
so that I can keep going.

Dog #2 teaches me how to love without conditions.

The third black Lab...

Days after joining our family,
this pooch runs right off the edge
of the patio's four-foot-high retaining wall.
I scoop the heft of puppy pudge
from the green summer lawn
and prod her with feather-like fingers,
searching for injury.
Henrietta is fine.
Apparently,
daredevil angels can take a licking and keep on ticking.

On a summer day,
she catches a rabbit
and squeezes the life out of it
between her jaws
while aghast and impotent, I watch.

Nine times out of ten,
if you toss her a treat,
it'll bounce off of her nose or sail by her ear.

Henrietta would give a cheetah a run for its money in a race.

This *fourleg* doesn't like to be touched
and avoids eye contact.
She likes to roll in the grass, the mud, and the snow.
She's a comedian who slinks like a cat.

Shake-my-head stories...
Swear and shout stories...
Unconditional love stories...
Living stories...
Henrietta teaches me what I need to learn
so that I can keep going.

Dog #3 teaches me what embracing my wild nature looks like.

GAIL
and her Joy

Image: Marijke van Veldhoven

And I wonder...
Who sends us the dog
that we need
instead of the dog
that we want?

3

PANORAMIC

By whose authority I cannot recall... the arborist came and wrote a do-not-disturb list. There's an Eastern red cedar outside our kitchen window that was saved from the chainsaw when it was added to an inventory of trees which we were mandated to work around when digging, building, and landscaping our new home.

A quarter century's flown by and there she still stands — her rawboned branches laden with blue cedar berries. I cannot say if the tree was ever aesthetically attractive, and I don't know how old she is, but the sway of her leaves seems to acknowledge my presence. Since we have come into each other's awareness, her sparse branches have always reminded me of an octogenarian's combover.

In the early years of our relationship, my appreciation and respect for her was like that of a twenty-something, which I was at the time, who thought she knew all about the world and what was necessary in it. Over the decades I've grown to understand, and to forgive, my misplaced arrogance.

And I wonder...

If my will had reigned, where would the beautiful flocks of cedar waxwings that now join me for breakfast dine?

4

FLASHBACK

Yesterday, a memory shook loose
when the Silverado kissed the garage's cedar siding.

Back in the 80s,
when I was as fresh to driving
as the pie I just pulled from the oven,
I was party to the screeching of brakes,
followed by the sickening sound
of metal meeting metal
in an unanticipated way.

Standing on the street corner
with tears streaming down my face,
I had no idea what had happened.

My view was unobstructed —
I had braked the orange Ford Pinto
to a full stop
as the sign directed.
I thought I had looked both ways,
but somehow I managed to T-bone a Chevy Nova
that was following the rules of the road to a tee.

Despite broken glass and bent metal,
somehow all flesh and bone escaped injury.

The grandmotherly lady
from the house on the corner
called my father at work.

Then something truly mind blowing happened:
My father arrived...
and kept his cool?

This unexpected outcome left a pleasing mark...
because now as I stare
at the dent on the side of the kid's pick-up,
I'm able to hold my composure.

And I wonder...
Are our trips, tumbles, and crashes
opportunities to learn
from the unforeseen?

5

EMPOWER

Nibbling a rough edge of my nail, I find myself lost for a response to the photos in front of me.

A friend wants my opinion regarding her mother-of-the-groom gown possibilities.

We have a long history as confidants since the days of homecoming, Sadie Hawkins, and prom dresses for dances.

I look at the images of my petite pal in oversized taffeta and silk that needs tailoring to accentuate the beauty of her small frame.

What does she see when she looks in the mirror?

How does the fabric feel?

Are there any scratches, pinches, or drooping straps to distract her presence as she celebrates crossing the threshold into mother-in-law-hood?

All of these are questions that could be asked, but fail to appear when needed.

I want to be helpful...

I want to show interest...

I want to be a good friend...

and yet —

I believe she knows which dress she prefers.

I believe my opinion will only serve to confirm or confuse.

I hesitate... and ask, "Which dress do you like best?"

And I wonder...

How often do I give advice when empowering someone to follow their own insight would be a better choice?

6

COMPOSED

Aware she risks ridicule
for her chosen route or lack of driving prowess,
she holds her spot behind the wheel.

This is one time
when her expectations and reality collide head on.

"Why didn't you turn there?"

She stays quiet...
and maintains a confident posture.

"The other way is faster."

She finds she's bold enough
to toss in a tiny challenge.
"Is this way... wrong?"

"No."

She offers a little charm

as they pass a farm…

"Going this way, we get to see the baby calves!"

Fully present and conscious
of what is transpiring,
she ponders…
Who is this self-assured creature inhabiting my body?

And I wonder…
Is practicing presence and awareness
poetry in motion?

7

POSTURE

Twenty-two years
within the scope of eternity
is invisible to the naked eye —
unless, of course,
it is your own eyes,
or God's,
that are doing the looking.

My first year as a mother
I'm given a certificate
that entitles me
to choose a pampering service
at a local spa.

Happy Mother's Day!

A pampering service is intriguing to one who is determined to grin and bear, pander and please... one who has resolved to dedicate her life to morphing into whatever a person, place, or thing demands... especially now, as she binds her life to that tiny flame of eternity that came through her.

Are children essential to spiking the love necessary for the world to survive our human pettiness, selfishness, and penchant for a good fight?

Recently, I read an article about a Russian botanist named Nikolai Vavilov who dedicated his life to ending famine. Although in boyhood he was sufficiently nourished, he heard stories of his ancestors dying of hunger. He also watched those less fortunate than himself perish around him for lack of food.

He complained about starvation and inequality through creativity — collaborating with nature via the science of genetics. Vavilov dedicated his life to building a seed bank of hardy plants.

Ironically, power, politics, and the inability to match a dictator's time-line relegated Valivov to a prison camp, where he died of... starvation.

I find myself vexed by the way the world sometimes treats her most dedicated servants.

Back to the spa where I stand on personal experience...

I note that the masseuse who escorts me to a dimly lit, lavender-scented room walks as if her spine is made of bamboo — a mix of straight-strength and flexibility.

Once I'm disrobed and lying face-up on her table, she asks me to relax and presses my shoulders to meet the white sheet underneath me. My rhomboid, trapezius, and serratus comply until her gentle pressure is released. Like well-trained soldiers, my muscles spring back into their habitual C shape, circling my heart.

"Relax? Please."

"I am relaxed."

After much kneading, squeezing, and stroking, the massage therapist escorts me to a lounge where cucumbers and strawberries float in sweating carafes of water.

"Continue to work at loosening up your shoulders, okay?" she suggests before calling her next client.

This young woman has no idea of the work, both physical and mental, that lies in store for me.

Twenty-two-ish years later...

On a morning walk, I note that an old house has installed a new chicken-eggs-for-sale stand at the end of their driveway. The scent of soap and dryer sheets tells me that somebody has initiated an early morning start on their laundry. The noise of a pump truck emptying a septic tank momentarily captures my attention.

Also, I note that the vertebrae in my neck have space between them, as if my head is being lifted by an invisible helium balloon. My shoulder blades rest comfortably on my back. There is a tautness to my abs. My spine has the strength and flexibility of bamboo.

And I wonder...

To accomplish anything meaningful in this world, are reinvention and rebirth integral facets of the game?

8

STRIKING

Striking,
creative, and unique —
words that describe the feelings
jumping up and down
on the wires
between my brain and heart.

My eyes drink
in the expressive structure.

No, I'm not talking about the Eiffel Tower,
the Sydney Opera House,
or the Leaning Tower of Pisa.

Humans build with materials —
tangible *and* abstract.

What's got me swooning is a poem
constructed with letters, words, and ideas.

The poet draws readers
through the verse's front door
with an architectural flourish
I've not seen before.

She makes the first sentence
of her poem
its title.

I've heard
there is nothing new under the sun,
yet there are endless things
new to me.

Like a backhoe excavating a site
for creative raising,
I dig it!

A short time
after discovering the poet's creative artistry,
at the library,
a book beckons to me
from the shelf.
Its rich cover hums,
"Step inside and have a look around."

Standing in the aisle,
surrounded by countless words and works
strung together with great care,
I open *this* book

to find an entire historical novel...
written in verse!

The part of me
that believes I am not abundant enough
with words
to write a novel
is now called in for questioning.
I'm curious enough
to check out the book.

Over the next several days,
I read the vibrance inside the jewel-tones
and marvel at what has just become a new possibility
in my mind's eye.

And I wonder...
What's possible
when we build with materials
that energize us?

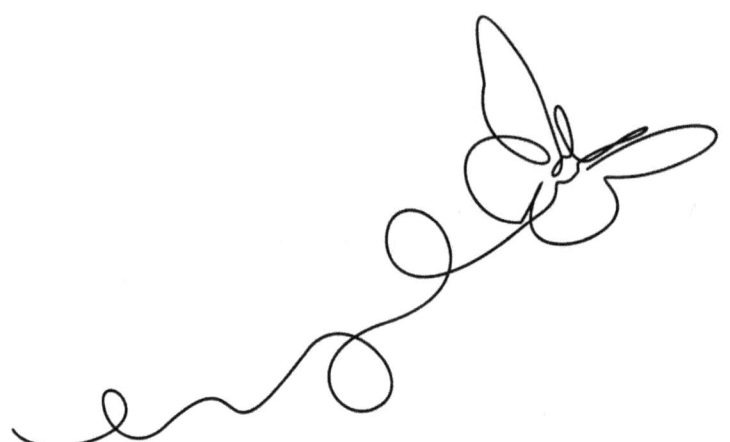

9

ENLIGHTEN

Five reminders arrive
within a twenty-four hour window.

Got it!
I got it.
Yup, I'm aware.
Sigh...
Delete.

The online conversation has been penciled
onto the top half of the day's square
for weeks.

Having exercised, showered, and broken fast,
I feel on top of my game.
Not only do I intend to listen and learn,
I hope for an opportunity to shine —
if only just a twinkle.

What's that?

I spy my right-hand dog panting and pacing
at the bottom of the stairs.

"What's wrong girl?
Need to go outside?"

Coat, boots, collar, leash —
we beat a path to the wild edge
where mowed lawn ends and brambles begin.

Eating grass.
Eating grass.
Eating grass.

"Your belly?
Are you trying to make yourself throw up?"

Tick, tick, tick.
"I'm gonna be late."

Presence.
"I know my priorities,
and you, my dear dog, have top billing."

The minutes go uncounted
as my fleece zip-up and the dog's fur coat
absorb the day's fog.
I attempt to drag seventy pounds of stubborn
toward the door.
The effort is an utter failure...
until I promise a truck ride.

Labrador loads.
I pop into the house for my keys and note the time
which is now quarter past the hour.
I'm too late to be fashionable and...
my *priority* waits for me to honor my word.

The ten-minute drive
to the park
is uneventful despite my internal
cursing for not thinking to grab a towel.
What if she pukes on the back seat?

At the park, our pace is... normal?
The *fourleg* does not nip or chew a single blade of grass.

My priority and I cross paths
with a man who mumbles
in response to my *Hello*,
yet does not raise his eyes
from the pavement
until my dog breaches the etiquette of personal space.

I pull back on her leash.
The man reaches out and wiggles his fingers
into damp fur.
He looks up and smiles
as he and *Fourleg* playfully touch and dodge one another.

And I wonder...
Was it the dog's twinkle
that was meant
for today's top billing all along?

10

VALUE

I see you, Anger —
red
behind my eyes.

Upheaval roams my intestines
reminding me of that sensation
when your child vomits
and for hours or days
your mind and body collude
in a game of *am I next?*

I hear your staccato

beating like high heels on tile,
a hammer hitting a nail.

I taste your rancor
in the burnt granola
that I've left far too long
in the oven.

I smell your sour
woven into the dog's collar
that hangs limp
on the hook in the entryway.

I watch your jerky movements
without reacting.

Anger,
you have my attention.
I know you are here
as a catalyst for change.

And I wonder...
How long will it take
for me to unite my sensitivities and sensibility
into a course of action?

11

WASTE NOT

The clank of heavy-duty glass on granite
nabs my attention.

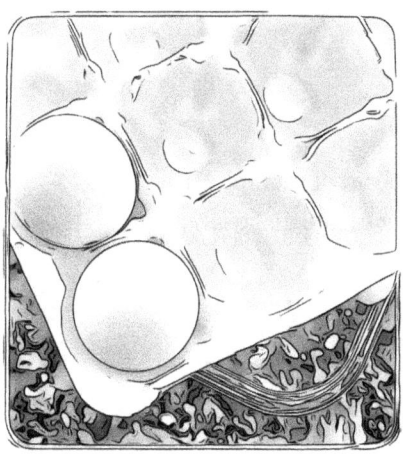

I look up as the depositing hand
grabs a carton of eggs from the refrigerator.

Ground beef, black beans, corn, tomatoes, and onions glare
at... me?

I suppose we're off to the trash now?

"You forgot to refrigerate your food again?"
I ask the egg-scrambler.

"Yes. I'm starving."

Quicker than egg whites solidify
when contacting hot metal, memories fire —

Starving African children with flies on their faces flash
across the console television screen of my childhood.

A stern food-safety class instructor warns
Better safe than sick.

My Southwest-soup-loving taste buds call,
Blasphemy!

My intestines scream,
Don't eat it!

Do I hear the sound of metaphorical coins
grinding in the garbage disposal?
Money down the drain?

Tick-tock goes the clock
as the scent of scrambled eggs
mingles with the taste of dark coffee.

And I wonder...
What are the possibilities if I stop perseverating,
throw out the soup,
wash the dishes,
and get on with my day?

12

TIMELY

The door's glass panel rattles.

Normally, I keep my eyes closed once I'm seated, but the rustle and bustle of the latecomer lifts my right eyelid to half mast. I taste a twinge of sour feelings at the sight of catalog-perfection. A neon-yellow tee tops off form-fitting leggings printed with lemons and limes. Dark curls cascade and bounce. Through one slitty eye I spy mani-cured fingers and toes, dressed in a coat of pale pink.

Bare feet slap against wood plank flooring. A citrus scent swirls around me as the student makes her way through rows of mats and yogis. Our instructor breaks away from the Hindu tale she's been sharing about Hanuman, a divine being who leapt for the sun thinking it was a ripe piece of fruit.

"Welcome. Please grab a block, a blanket, and a strap."

I resist the urge to turn and look when I hear several blocks in the prop room tumble to the floor. My monkey mind leaps between *how rude* and *namaste*. The raucous unfurl of a yoga mat behind my left shoulder gives *how rude* the upper hand.

"So, Hanuman broke his jaw," Sarah resumes. "Tonight we'll be working towards hanumanasana — split pose."

Throughout class I work to expand my strength and flexibility. I inhale and exhale, salute the sun, and turn my gaze within. I find that doing the splits is still an intention to work toward. While focusing on my practice, I completely forget about the tropical beauty behind me.

My fellows and I roll up our mats and return the props to the black wire shelving along the back wall.

I overhear the latecomer speaking to our teacher. In stark contrast to the inner calm I feel, the woman's words pinball like a tin of marbles spilled through the ceiling — something about work, her "stupid" back, and the limited parking available near the studio.

Sarah's response is like a babbling brook conveying care, calm, and interest. *How did you injure yourself? Do you sit or stand a lot during the day?*

Sarah turns to self-vulnerability as a guide... "*I have chronic tightness and pain in my shoulders and neck. When I keep up with practice and view my body's signals as a teacher for my mind, I'm able to frame the pain in a different light. Instead of feeling angry, I'm grateful.*"

I exit the glass paneled door hoping that I'll see the long brown curls again.

Namaste comes out on top.

And I wonder...

Did this new student actually arrive right on time?

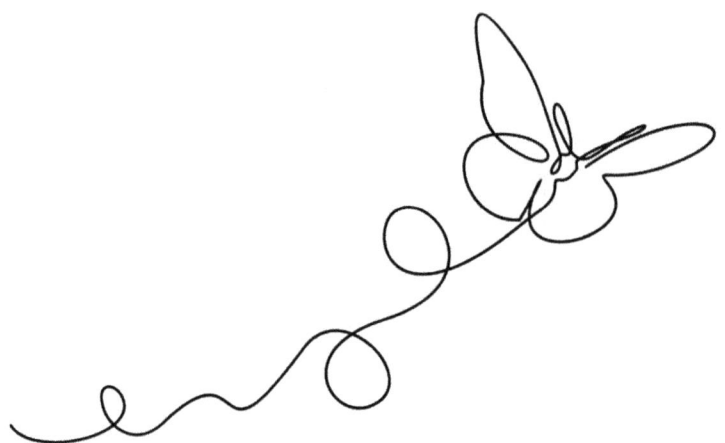

13

EXCHANGE

As my truck's tires transition their trajectory from west to north, I spy a smile protruding into the middle of the road. Something's amiss. I consider the irritation of the drivers behind me as my speed mirrors the pace of a woolly bear caterpillar. My cautious nature trumps my desire to people-please.

Yup. Amiss. That Amazon van's front end is stuck in the ditch. The orange smile on the navy van seems unperturbed.

I inch past flashing tail lights, slow, stop, and turn on my truck's hazards. I look both ways before opening my door and shuffling back to the carrier of coffee makers, books, toilet paper, and just about anything else money can buy.

At my approach, the driver rolls down the van's window. "Hey!"

"Everything okay? Are you hurt?"

"Nah — I'm fine," the driver replies, "Just waiting on a tow."

"You're the third vehicle I've seen in a ditch between here and Moorland Boulevard. This year's first snowfall is like a wet bar of soap!"

"Yeah! It is! Just before I came here, I stopped to check on a lady. She said she wasn't going more than ten miles an hour and she just slid right off the road."

"Anything I can do for you?" I asked.

"Nah — I'll just wait. Tow trucks are busy today."

"You sure?"

"Yeah — get wherever you're going safely and thanks for stopping to check on me."

"You bet. Take care of you!"

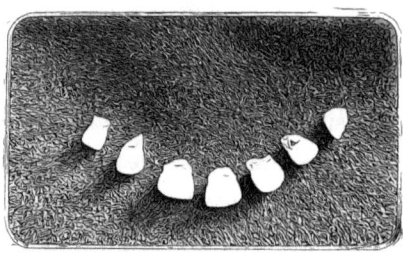

If the Amazon driver and I were jars of jam, his label might have a picture of a smiling strawberry, mine...a smiling grape. Despite all our differences, both smiles are missing a tooth, which makes my smile grow even bigger. Seems to me we both recognize that when it comes to jam, the labels aren't what we eat. We're after the sweet stuff inside.

And I wonder...

Is every conversation an opportunity?

14

PROVIDENCE

Something in the winter night moves as I shift from drive to park. *Coyotes?* I hesitate to open my truck's door. And then I see a human head — two... three. The coyotes are people! It's my neighbor Andy and his kids, Bri and Ethan. I hop out of the truck and am greeted by the sound of laughter. The trio knows they have surprised me.

"What are you guys up to?"

"Sledding down the ditch! Want to have a go?" Andy extends his sled.

I *do* want to have a go, but I am wearing thin pants and dress boots. "Nah, not dressed for it. Another time? I wish I'd have thought of ditch sledding when my kid was little!"

"We were sledding on our side of the street the night it snowed. It got too icy over there, so we asked if we could sled on this side." Andy motions toward the Snyder's house. Their ditch runs from the corner, along the side yard, past our bank of rural mailboxes, and ends at the driveway to my house. "This side is a little steeper — and longer."

The sun has set hours ago. On my drive home, my thoughts are on dinner, followed by a snuggle with a fleece blanket on the couch. This stop to grab our mail grants me an unexpected gift of warm connection. "You guys know how to have fun!"

"Gotta keep 'em away from the computer and TV somehow."

"I appreciate your effort — I know what a challenge that is! Have a great night." I climb back into the driver's seat, pull my door shut, and shift into drive.

And, I wonder...

Is parenting both the hardest and most joy-filled work on earth?

15

ACTIVATE

Heart and yeast are active, yet my spirit collapses onto a kitchen chair when I recognize what I've done. Was my brain active as it followed a well-worn pattern? Eeeee... I only meant to preheat the oven for dinner. In my failure to actively think, my failure to be present, my failure to see the implements of bread-making strewn across the countertop... I punched the bake button, set the temp to 350°F, and pressed the start key to fire the oven.

Five minutes later, a baker leaves his televised football playoff game to fold the bread dough one final time before transferring the seeded whole-wheat loaves into cast iron Dutch ovens for baking. He opens the oven door to find dough cooking before its time.

The plastic storage container is melted and is stuck fast to the metal oven rack.

Gulp!

"I'm so sorry!" I didn't mean..." I stammer.

After he spent a full day gathering ingredients, mixing, kneading, and tending, I see disappointment and anger duel with *I know it was an accident* on the baker's face.

"It's just that I spent all day."

"I know you did. I'm truly sorry. I was operating on my default system."

"Yes."

"Next time you use the warmth of the oven light to aid your dough's rise, will you please place a sticky note on the oven controls?"

"I already thought of that. Yes."

And I wonder...

When we feel like a failure or when we stumble, are we being asked to rise?

16

TABLED

How many muscles contract to pull a mouthful of *chunky monkey* through a straw?

Ice-cold milk, blended with bananas, chocolate, and peanut butter rise at my commanding sip. Fingering a hot pink straw, I marvel for a moment at bodily functions I often take for granted. I suck, swallow, and savor as my tablemates catch up on the happenings in their lives since we last met.

Stories circulate around the table square about grandchildren, health concerns for aging parents, employment triumphs and concerns, and then... We're on to the travel news — where we've been, where we're going, and where we plan to go after that. As I visualize verbal snap-shots of cruises and fjords, tropical beaches, and renditions of *Mama Don't Let Your Babies Grow Up to Be Cowboys* on Nashville rooftops, I'm aware my turn is coming...

Where have I been?

Where am I going?

Well that's a million-dollar question because my current life adventure is a full effort in self-study — in trading up the fit-in, go-along-to-get-along woman I've been for becoming my truest, best self.

"The marsh. I spend a lot of time walking near the marsh," I say when it's my turn. This is such a seemingly dull adventure that I'm allowed to slip back into solitary sipping.

And I wonder...

Would they understand if I said "I've been growing where I'm planted"?

17

SATISFY

Through glass smudged with Labrador nose prints, I watch winter sun rays refract their light into tiny rainbows upon freshly fallen snow. Even though the morning temperature is sub-zero, I overhear a cardinal speak of spring from the top of the birch outside our front door.

"Good morning, Mr. Cardinal," I call through the wall before turning to head upstairs to polish myself for the day ahead. And that's when I spy... different winter sun rays dancing on a stairway cobweb.

Underneath the glistening, untidy strands, there are a few dog hairs and a tiny pebble. Instead of swiping away the incriminating evidence of neglectful housekeeping, I snap a photo and follow my curiosity. I ask the search engine:

What is the difference between a spiderweb and a cobweb?

It turns out that a cobweb is an abandoned spider's web... It collects dust and dirt over time. Whether the spider vacated before or after the pebble and dog hair appeared is anybody's guess.

Where has the spider gone?

I suspect it has a new address somewhere on the staircase.

And I wonder...

When did I notice that there's something to learn from pests of all kinds?

18

DECIDE

"C'mon!" my *self* nags me while standing for uncounted minutes in front of a display of paper napkins.

"I like the clover pattern..." a dialogue, exclusive to my own head, picks up, "and the beverage size is only $2.99 for thirty-six. That's less than 10 cents each."

I watch my *self* pick up the full-size, cellophane-wrapped bundle of the same pattern, turn it over to reveal the $4.99 price tag, and set it back down. "The cocktail size will work for our craft project," says one of my many muses.

"Yes, and... we really only need one or two from the pack. Wouldn't it be better —" I hear another muse suggest.

Another cuts her off, "to buy the dinner size? We have no use for beverage napkins. What's two more dollars?"

"Maybe, but you know we only pull out fancy napkins for guests. We prefer the soft bargain napkins from the grocery," argues a muse.

I watch myself hold the squares in my right hand and the rectangles in my left. I set them both back on the shelf before taking a few steps toward the exit.

"You have got to be kidding me!" a muse stops me, and I stand on tiles of indecision to duke it out. "We came to this store on our way home from the library specifically to get napkins for the project —" she continues.

I'm really quite good at cutting my *self* off because one muse interrupts, "Correction! To in-ves-tigate, not get."

After an audible sigh, "They only cost 2.99."

"They'll probably go on sale after St. Patrick's Day?" throws a muse.

"They'll be gone after St. Patrick's Day. Please pick them up and go to the register," decides a determined muse.

"Should we?" I ask.

"Yes!" they all reply.

We stand in the check out line, make it to the register, and finalize the purchase.

And I wonder...

When did I get so good at giving my attention to all my muses and the art of personal negotiation?

19

ADMISSION

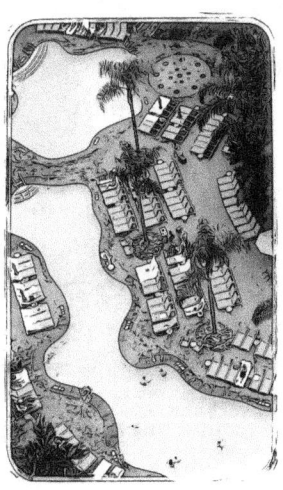

Sultry and sunny weather calls a long line of people to purchase a ticket. We wind our way toward a sign that proclaims *World's Largest Waterpark*, awaiting our turn to splash and scream with those on the other side of the fence.

I wade deeper and deeper as my mom radar persistently scans the sea of humanity for a boy with my features in this sea of water, as he enjoys his time in the pool.

Wet and refreshed, our group steps from the rollicking breakers to explore what other sensory delights the waterpark has to offer. What child wouldn't want a thirty-six-ounce, lime-green, refillable cup with bendable straw? Sipping at enough fizzy soda to pop the eyes and minds of tiny bodies, we watch the brave leap off of sky-high bouncy boards. Our entire group nods a communal headshake of *No, thanks*.

On a ride called the Stingray, a raft full of thrill seekers is released for a quick descent followed by an ascent that threatens to catapult them into the sky above. *Not for us.*

Ohhh, look! A young friend thinks he's found his adventure. "C'mon" he cries to his mother.

"Will you join us?" she asks me and my son.

This flavor of amusement is well outside of both our comfort zones. Cautious by nature, we size up the monstrous slide accentuated with three gargantuan drop-offs. This will push us beyond our limit, but the boy and I nod and agree. "Sure, we'll do it."

Our foursome zig-zags up... and up... and up. The queue is vast and slow-moving, which offers us much time to fret over our decision to ride. Just a few stairs from the top, our young catalyst for the climb loses his verve. Unbelievable to me, my boy wonder holds strong and we watch our friends' backs as they wind their way down against traffic until it's our turn to board a yellow raft and face our fears.

Clutching the handles of the life raft and willing the experience to end, we arrive at the bottom in under a minute's time. I'm not ashamed to speak my truth. For seconds that felt like hours, I was terrified — for myself — and more so for my offspring. *Was he holding the handles tightly enough?* Looking into each other's faces, I note that the arrangement of our facial features matches. This is what terror looks like.

We get out of the raft. My insides are jelly. My brain commands my legs to move. I breathe and attempt to settle my nervous system back to equilibrium. Aware that my role as mother is to be strong and chipper, I manage to muster, "That wasn't so bad, now was it? It was fun even."

I'm a terrible, unbelievable liar. I can feel the kid reading the truth in my eyes. He knows what I felt and reads me like a favorite book. Aware, I follow up with, "I hated it!"

"Me, too," he echoes, "but we did it!"

And I wonder…

What is gained and lost in courage born from vulnerability?

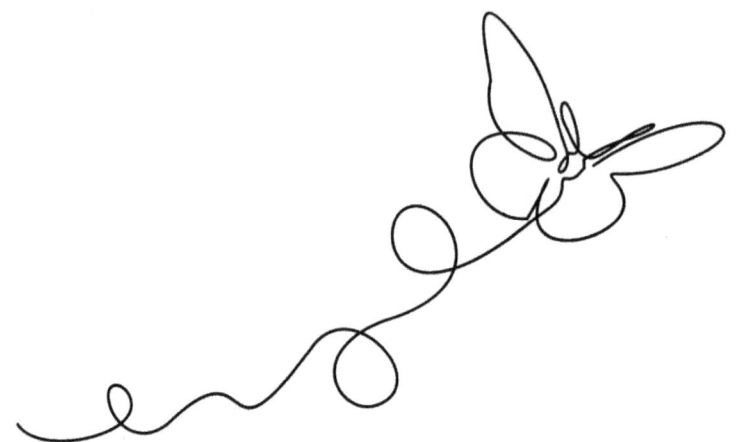

20

HARVEST

Unlock the plastic zipper and pour.
Clinkety-tinkety...
deep purple frozen black raspberries
make a statement
accentuated by white porcelain.

A thirty-second spin in the microwave
and voila! —
cereal and milk mix and mingle
with last summer's harvest
for today's breakfast.

Now — take a seat at the table
by the window.

Outside, bare branches hugged
by hoar frost sparkle,
as warm, forced air plucks away
the shiver in your slippers.

And even though single-digit Fahrenheit seeps
through terracotta-hued walls
while holiday lights twinkle on the mantle,
you're pretty sure July will come 'round again...

Deer flies will buzz and bite.
Beads of sweat will roll
down the back of your neck.
Brambles will scratch and draw blood
while you harvest the tasty reminder
that seasons come
and seasons go.

And I wonder...
Where else
might I harvest the sweetness of one season
to enjoy in another?

21

THE ART OF CHANGE

We were newly married and childless — and had time on our hands. When my husband suggested we sign up for a Taekwondo class through our city's recreation department, I hesitated. I'd never considered myself *Karate Kid* material. Wisconsin winters are filled with short days and long dark nights and so with nothing better to do than watch *Entertainment Tonight* while sharing the sofa with our cat, I thought *why not?*

We arrived early to our first class in the basement of city hall. I wore 1990s-style sweatpants — the kind that had elastic cuffs at the bottom and are now back in vogue — and a souvenir sweatshirt from Volendam, Holland. The soft, light blue cotton sported an outline of a windmill in navy ink. We figured it was best to get a few classes under our belts before investing in any traditional martial arts' attire.

As the rest of our classmates began filing in, I noticed some were still young enough to be gripping their parents' hands? *Boy — was I glad I hadn't been too gung-ho about our attire.* Turns out we were the only adults participating in the training. Moms and dads sat on plastic chairs around the perimeter of the room while our instructor taught us how to correctly throw a punch.

Beyond my initial unease and embarrassment, what I remember from the experience is that we attended every class of the six-week session and that the primary purpose of a martial art is self-defense. This art hinges on discipline.

And I wonder...

When we change ourselves, do we change the world?

22

PROVOCATION

Sweat trickles down my back as I squat. Dappled shade from hickory and walnut trees offers checkered relief from the blazing sun but does nothing to soften the humidity. Gloved, my thumb and index finger pinch and pull, pinch and pull. Weed by weed I drop purslane, clover, and thistle into an orange five-gallon bucket. This might sound strange, but I enjoy clearing a flower bed of weeds. It's peaceful, honest work. I can look back and see what I've accomplished — a simple pleasure with an observable result.

On this particular day, though, my peace is interrupted. At first, it is just one bee buzzing by my ear. I swish at it with my hat and keep on pinching and pulling until the lone buzzer enlists friends. Soon several are circling me. Well aware grumpy bees will sting, I do the logical thing: I run. The drones follow me at a you're-on-our-radar-but-we-are-not-looking-for-a-fight speed. They break off when I enter the garage. Unscathed and undeterred, I wait a few minutes before heading back to my bucket. Pinch, pull, pinch, pull... *What?!*

More bees. Run, hide, wait, repeat. Sometimes I'm a little slow to catch on to things. The third time I return to the bucket, the bees don't even give me time to squat. Thankfully, I have enough smarts to take off my garden gloves and head into the house for some lunch.

Mid-afternoon, from a safe distance, I watch bees bumbling about in the area of my morning's effort. For hours I sneak peeks as they fly above the rich brown dirt looking for the entrance to their nest. Ahhh! I now understand. These are ground bees and I must have disturbed their peace by shaking up their home.

My dad once shared a schoolboy story with me. He grew up in the country and completed grades one through eight in a one-room schoolhouse. Among his schoolmates, there was a big boy named Deloy, who had a reputation for shaking things up with the other kids.

Slow to finish his lunch one day, my dad asked the teacher if he could finish his pear outside at recess. Exiting the door, he saw Deloy sitting atop his bicycle, pedaling hard, with the kickstand down.

"Deloy, get off my bike!"

"Make me."

When the pear struck his cheek, Deloy dismounted and came at my dad whose smallness and quickness turned out to be an advantage in the short fight that ensued. Summoned by the girls, the lone schoolhouse teacher soon put a stop to the jabs, weaves, swings, and ducks.

Looking at the larger boy's bleeding face, she asked my dad, "Roger, did you do this?"

"Yes."

"C'mon Deloy," she guided, "Let's go get you cleaned up."

As the story goes, Miss Kreft didn't say another word about the altercation... and my dad and Deloy never had another problem between them.

Nothing happens in a vacuum.

Our actions — and our responses to the actions of others and our environment — ripple out into the world.

And I wonder...

Can attentive awareness of our *selves* and how we show up save us from some of life's stings?

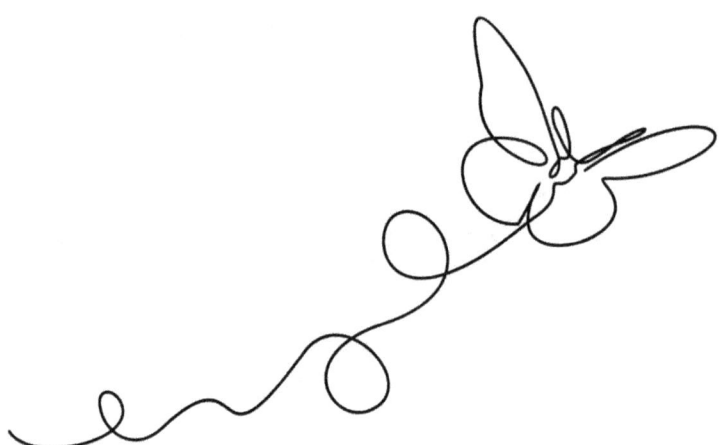

23

INTRICACIES

"It's just nature!" I snap in a tone that elicits feelings of discomfort.

A snake swims by the dock where our feet dangle in lukewarm lake water. Its head and neck are wide, tapering near mid body. Inside of my mind I hear: *If they could set aside disgust and fear, they'd notice that the snake's skin is tan with dark brown markings. They'd observe how the snake glides through the water, not in a straight line, but twisting and swirling.*

On reflection, I know my friends' reaction is more *normal* than mine. In the past, I would have kept quiet or even feigned fear myself? I mean, we're supposed to be afraid of and disgusted by spiders and snakes, aren't we? Everybody knows this. But why? The vast majority are harmless and quite fascinating.

A little later that same afternoon, a dead, rotting, stink-up-the-shore-line fish floats near enough for us to pinch our noses closed.

"Nature!" one of my friends cries out in jest. "It's just nature!" We all laugh while she swishes the fish down the shoreline.

A week later, walking together, we take note of mating dragonflies, spiders and their webs, milkweed plants sustaining Monarch butterflies, and wild blackberries on thorny vines along the ditch verge. Every time we focus on something from our natural surroundings, one of us whoops, "Nature!"

I'm certain I haven't converted my friends into naturalist wannabes, but maybe sharing a piece of my emotionally-charged self has helped us to connect with each other and with nature? Maybe next time they'll pause to think about spider feet feeling vibrations through silken fibers before sucking up an intricate web with a vacuum attachment?

And I wonder...

What happens when my thinking shifts from *this is right and that is wrong* to *I see and hear you; do see and hear me, too*?

24

WHENEVER I FEEL AFRAID

The frog doesn't make haste toward the tall riverbank grasses at my approach, so I crouch and send a silent message: *I'm not going to hurt you. Let's share a moment.*

Blink. I slowly raise my phone, expecting him to bolt.

Already this morning, several Monarch butterflies, numerous frogs, and a snail have played shy to my lens. While I kneel within the distance of a hopscotch toss, the frog doesn't twitch, flinch, or blink. I wonder for a flash — is the amphibian a fake? An errant fishing lure?

Then, my black, furry *fourleg* ambles past without noticing the frog. The frog senses the dog. Its yellow throat and stomach bulge and retract. *You're brave!* I think of the frog. *She stepped within inches of you and you didn't leap for cover.*

Emboldened myself, I creep within arms length and snap a close-up. If I uncurled my index finger, I could touch *Braveheart. How do you like that nickname, Frog? Are you as curious about me as I am about you?*

In a flash, the spell is broken as a wet black nose comes in for a sniff. *Braveheart* can no longer deny her instinct. With one powerful thrust from her rear legs, she's gone.

Nice to meet you! I called.

And I wonder...

Did I just receive a lesson in courage... from a frog?

25

MOVING FORWARD, WALKING BACKWARDS

Frozen. The truck's thermometer reads sixteen degrees Fahrenheit. Wind lifts my bangs. I open the back door and four paws dismount with gymnastic aplomb. We head down a gravel trail into the marsh — a choice outside of our usual path. This section of trail is heavily wooded and provides some relief from Mother Nature's biting blasts. I'm not surprised to find we have the place to ourselves.

I'm in no mood for dawdling and hold a steady pace while glancing over my shoulder to check on my strolling accomplice. For stretches, I turn and walk backwards in an effort to give my watering eyes respite from the day's gusts. I ponder the life metaphor of physically walking backwards while making forward progress.

It feels like going somewhere without being able to see the destination. Not seeing, I listen closely. I cultivate faith in my senses and intuition to guide each backward, forward progression. Can I trust my strength, agility, and balance? Will these qualities keep me upright if I misstep or collide with an obstacle?

And I wonder...

Does walking backwards while moving forward kindle a sense of adventure in my soul?

26

SHARPEN

A slight pull on the brushed nickel handle and my digits are rambling through a junk drawer that holds every kind of catchall kitsch. Among loose nails, paper clips, rubber bands and blue ink pens, I pinch what I came for — a full-length, sunshine-yellow #2 Ticonderoga with a supple pink eraser — the best and most reliable pencil known to any kindergarten teacher.

After a bit more digging, I pick up a navy two-holed sharpener between my thumb and index, insert the pencil's dull end, then twist-turn-twist until the graphite tip pleases my sense of *just right.*

I settle myself at the kitchen table with a legal pad, my telephone, the pencil, and a mug of Earl Grey. Next, I tap the *return call* button after listening to a voicemail — *Hi Gail. It's Dad.* He says that every single time... as if I wouldn't recognize his voice. I smile and resist saying *duh* out loud.

Just called to talk. Today is the day your mother and I got married sixty years ago. It was a beautiful day. Hope to talk to you soon.

Whew! There's no emergency.

This is the kind of voicemail you answer when you can offer undivided attention. You sharpen a pencil, grab a notebook, and prepare to forget about time. For forty minutes, Dad and I fuse past and present. I ask questions I've never asked before. The greatest gift I can give to my eighty-two-year-old father is an attentive listening ear. In every conversation I make an effort to paint the story of our history together as a grand adventure. I want him to hear that he's played a great role in shaping a good daughter.

"So tell me about October 11, 1958?"

"It was warm and sunny — a beautiful October day."

I want to know how he felt when Mom started down the aisle. I can hear the smile in his voice — envision it on his face — when he says *proud*.

His word choice delights me, but also catches me off guard. He always told me that pride is a sin. I've come to believe there are no sinful feelings; it's how we act on our emotions that matters. In my mind's eye, I see the wedding picture that hung in my parents' bedroom, their hands together, poised to cut the cake.

"Mom was so pretty and spirited; I can see why you felt that way. Were you nervous?"

"Of course I was!"

I'm surprised to learn the reception hall was open to the public for the dance.

"That was fine because paying patrons offset our cost for the band. We were pretty poor, but we made do. Your grandfather was laid off from his job. There just wasn't a lot of money. Things are different everywhere now."

"Mom loved to dance, right?"

"She did," he replies." It's bothered me for my whole life — I just never could make my feet go together with the music. I always wished I could have done that for her — enjoyed dancing. That would have made her happy."

Had my father just slipped himself into my mother's proverbial dancing shoes?

"We opened our wedding gifts during the band's intermission. I never liked that," he shares. "It didn't seem right to open gifts in front of everyone. Somebody maybe gave you a nice set of dishes and then you'd open a broom and dust pan from somebody else who couldn't afford much of a gift. I didn't like how it might make the broom and dustpan giver feel — like they were less because they couldn't afford something better. People don't get married for the gifts."

My dad is thoughtful — in a way I never fully recognized until l made the time to really listen.

"Dad — I've got to get going. Tell me a joke?" I ask.

"What does a cow have four of that a lady only has two of?"

"Legs?"

"Well, yeah — but that's not the answer people usually give — hahaha! Funny how people's minds work!"

And I wonder...

Is the shaping of a meaningful life anything like sharpening a worthwhile pencil?

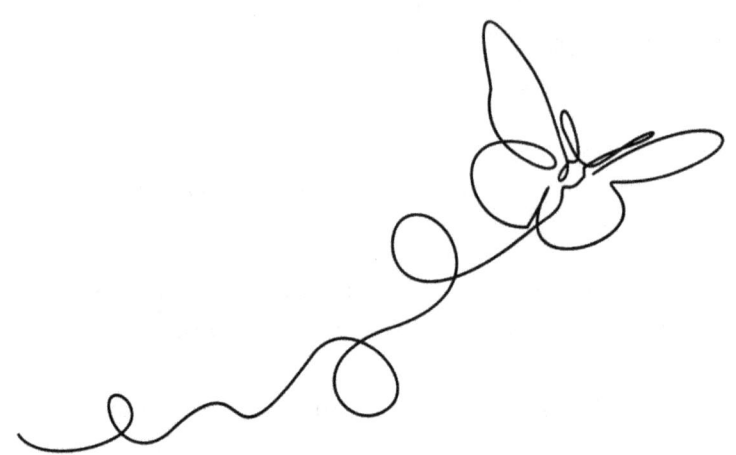

27

WHO'S THE TURKEY?

I can roll my eyes, but there are no noise-cancelling headphones for the racket in my head. On this peach of a Midwestern April day, my companion and I climb the hills and round the curves between her house and mine. Our pooches saunter, sniff, and occasionally stop to *scent* a message that they've passed this way.

As we enter the intersection of Isaw Road and Noway Lane, I listen to my companion's *incredible* story about a flock of turkeys attacking backpack-toting grade-schoolers at the bus stop.

Image by: KO Photography

One voice in my head — the eye roller — is in total disbelief. She's the loudest, calling from the bare back of a haughty, high horse. *Wild turkeys are not predators. Every wild turkey we have ever encountered has fled at our approach.* More than anything, this voice likes to be right.

Another voice in my head — the bridge builder — tries to make sense of this information.

Her gaze swivels from outside to inside. She looks for information to upset the high-horse's apple cart. *Did the turkeys have young? Were the children throwing rocks?*

Did they run at the birds?

A third voice — the introvert — grumbles. *Why do we insist on walking with other people when we could be walking by ourselves?*

A fourth intercedes. *How can we learn anything new if we shut ourselves off from the world?*

Number five — an observer of all the other voices – sighs.

And I wonder...

Why do we spend precious energy arguing over somebody else's perception of events we didn't even see with our own eyes?

28

ENTERTAIN

We met a goose named Georgie
at a local ice cream stand.
He arrived in a sky-blue pick-up truck —
his feathers white and grand.

Orange beak poked out the driver's window...
Upon his handler's lap he sat.
I had to do a double take;
That's no dog or cat!

In no time a crowd gathered
to gawk, engage, connect.
While owner bought a sundae,
Georgie stood erect.

Trash bin served as kingly perch
for this regal, pampered bird.
What on earth would he have said
if his thoughts could be heard?

Quirky carer returned with goodies
and tucked Georgie under his arm.
The pair then left for parts unknown —
probably a farm?

And I wonder...
Where in life do I
have the boldness
to be a nonconformist?

29

REVELATION

"No," he said. "I'm not going."

Wait... What?

When I first heard that the family patriarch was boycotting the summer trip to the lake, I thought exactly what I'd been conditioned to think, "How terrible! He's supposed to go, to build family memories, to be supportive. It won't be the same without him. He can't do that." That said... I don't particularly care for the annual trip myself.

Pack up half of the house, including bedding and pantry, load the truck, drive for hours, unload the truck, beach in whatever weather Mother Nature decides to deal, play games, swat at flies, mosquitos, and no-see-

ums, tour the town's tourist traps, pack up, drive home, unpack, run the washer and dryer for twenty-four hours straight, and file the packing list for next year's reference.

Predictable.

Safe.

A tradition?

When the vehicles are loaded and heading north, Grandpa holds to his word and stays with the dogs at home, where he has a functional television, a full-size shower, and a routine that he prefers.

A seed is planted. *So... I can really say no? People do that... and get away with it?* As calendar years roll one into the next, the lake tradition holds, as does the father's resolve not to participate. The seed sets roots and waits for the right conditions.

Small children grow into adult-sized bodies. We are now seven people sharing one miniature cabin with one miniature bathroom. I long for a new vacation experience.

I float the possibility. *What if... we do something different next year?*

Is it time? The suggestion is blasphemy to some. Others take the consideration to heart.

A new vista begins taking shape on the horizon.

And I wonder...

Where else in my life might this-is-no-longer-for-me unleash freedom?

30

REVERSAL

With our help, you, too, can be funny.

Imagine you earn a job promotion that requires you to train for three months away from home. You're one in a class of ten students, sitting two by two. Each seat comes with a computer, hefty manuals filled with dense legalese, paper, and pencils. You're put up in a hotel and given a substantial per diem. *Sweet, right?* You're gifted a break from your daily routines — free from office drudgery. Time in the big city on your employer's dime allows family to visit on weekends for mini-vacations.

Now, imagine your first day of class... One of the two instructors is young, fresh from a small town college campus. She already holds the position you have been promoted to but has worked for the agency for a mere fraction of the time you have – the perks of a diploma. Not exactly endearing, is she?

She introduces herself, outlines what she'll be teaching, and then says something like, "I can teach you the material, but I apologize in advance. I'm not really funny or entertaining, but I do have a solid understanding of the rules and regulations you need to learn." Pin-drop silence.

Under her bobbed cut, the young woman believes her eyes and ears actually see and hear minds clicking and ticking. *Perhaps this attempt at vulnerability was... a misstep?* Have you ever completely discounted yourself, pre-apologizing for your own perceived weaknesses?

With grace, a dozen people learned what it takes to overcome an inadequate introduction, enjoyed each other's company, and grew together. As a parting gift, the class gave the burgeoning instructor a custom printed t-shirt that read: *With our help, you, too, can be funny.*

And I wonder...

How often do I lock myself inside of an unlocked cage?

31

ETERNAL YOUTH

I'm three steps out of the kitchen when I hear the ruckus. *She only waited until I was three steps out of the kitchen?* I turn on my heel and growl, "Mara!" To anybody who can hear me upstairs I call, "This dog of ours will never grow up!"

Sure enough, a loaf of bread is on the floor. The thin plastic bag is torn and the bread thief has an entire slice of sourdough clamped between her jaws. My first grab is for the loaf, which I place on the counter. Second, I try to snatch the half slice still protruding from Mara's mouth, but she outflanks me and hauls heinie into the family room, where she swallows without chewing.

"What did you do?" I bark.

She looks *repentant* — which I suspect she is not. I'm not sure which one of us is the better actress in this little drama that plays out under the kitchen's overhead can lighting. If she really feels bad, she'll stop this foolishness. Bread, buns, and empty meat containers from the trash have all been snagged as edible props by the *fourleg*.

I'll let you in on a little secret — I'm tickled and amused that my ten-year-old sidekick still has the vim and vigor to act like a pup. I'm the one who needs to be more conscientious about keeping the bread out of reach and the trash emptied.

Kitchen sorted, my *fourleg* and I venture over to the marsh to walk off some carbohydrates. Our little corner of the world was kissed with winter's fluffiest precipitation overnight. Every branch, blade, pod, and spent seed head holds a dollop of nature's shaved ice. Lifeless Queen Anne's lace remnants form perfect funnel cups.

I take note, feel a pull, and say, "Nah." But there are hundreds, maybe even thousands, of bite-sized, pure white mounds that call to me. *"C'mon. You know you want to!"* I can no longer resist the temptation and walk up to a chin-high cone, tilt my head, and invite the crown of snowy fluff to melt on my tongue and lips.

Mara and I continue to explore the fields and I savor the sensation of at least fifteen to twenty more meltable mini-mounds. Each one delivers a Lilliputian thrill of presence. At one point, Mara eyeballs me, and I think I can read her thoughts: "She'll never grow up!"

And I wonder...

Where else in life might I give myself permission to enjoy simple pleasures?

32

UNSCRIPTED

Mark invites me to join a networking group that meets every other Tuesday morning for breakfast at a local restaurant. He's a semi-retired businessman who volunteers as a mentor for entrant entrepreneurs. Prior to starting my food manufacturing company, my experience in the working world has all been public service — clients and children showing up whether I want them to or not.

I've never before been challenged to sell a product or service. Doing so does not come naturally to me, and I'm certain Mark has his work cut out for him. "So, what happens at these meetings?" I ask.

"Well, sometimes we practice our elevator speeches — short version, long version. Usually one member is allocated extra time to elaborate on his/her business. Sometimes guest speakers attend."

"Do I need to bring anything?"

"You should definitely have your business cards and you might want to offer some samples of your product."

I will not lie. I am nervous that first morning and many of the following Tuesdays. I do not like pitching my product and sweat every time it's my turn to speak. Between bites of pancakes and sips of coffee, everyone else seems so comfortable.

A chiropractor extols the virtues of toxin removing foot baths. A loan officer gives updates on interest rates. A real estate agent keeps us updated on the local property market, and an accountant lets us know she's available to help us with our bookkeeping and tax filing needs. The people are always intriguing even though I often have little interest in what they're selling.

After a few meetings, I understand the real purpose of the group is to refer business to each other. I feel like a boot in a row of bananas, apples, and oranges on a which-of-these-does-not-belong worksheet, yet I'm determined to reciprocate the generosity of connection that has been offered to me. Also, I feel an obligation to provide value of some kind.

My idea for the next Tuesday morning meet up does not involve pitching my business. I'd recently read in a popular business book about the psychology of reciprocity. Humans, the author explained, are hardwired to reciprocate.

Instead of hawking maple-syrup sweetened seeds and nuts, I want to offer behavioral awareness that might help my fellow sellers to gain more customers, so I write my own script.

I spend days excitedly thinking about how best to present the information I've learned. I create a handout annotated with bullet points and inspirational quotes. I am a self-appointed professor who waits for her turn to speak with excitement, rather than anxiety. "Good morning. I'm Gail from Satisfying Snacks. Today I'm going to share a little something about the psychology of reciprocity."

I distribute my handouts and business cards, share my newfound knowledge, and close with, "Thank you for this opportunity to reciprocate the kindness you have shown by including me in your group."

What did my fellows think? I don't know for sure. I've learned what they think is their business, not mine.

And I wonder...

How often does an ill-fitting life exploration point us toward a better fit?

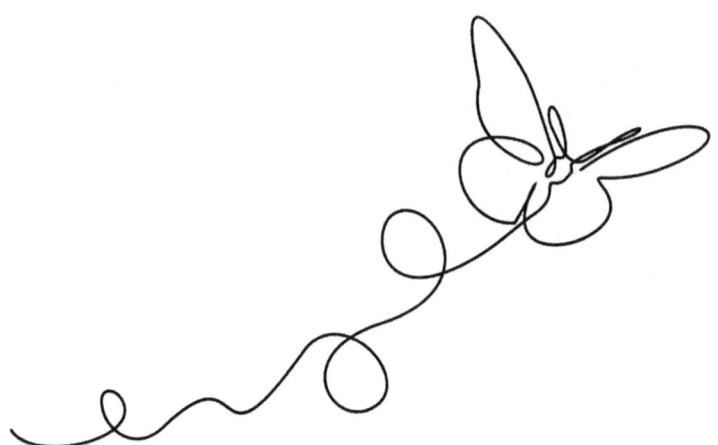

33

PRESS RELEASE

On a sunny, suburban, autumn afternoon, a puddle of coffee ice cream swallows a fly.

Yes, he dies.

Authorities announce they will not press charges in the case, although they agree there was neglect on the part of the ice cream devotee. Her bowl most certainly should have been rinsed and placed in the dish-washer, where it would not be a hazard. She has been issued a warning.

The fly's exact cause of death cannot be determined due to insufficient forensic evidence. The coroner proposes that sugar poisoning and/or wing saturation are likely culprits.

The fly leaves behind several friends and family members. They, too, are in danger of premature death as their irritating nature conjures homicidal urges in their two-legged housemates who swat at them with newspapers and dish towels.

In other news, weather reports call for nighttime temperatures to consistently dip below freezing.

And I wonder...

Is writing stories good for the soul?

34

THAT FEELING

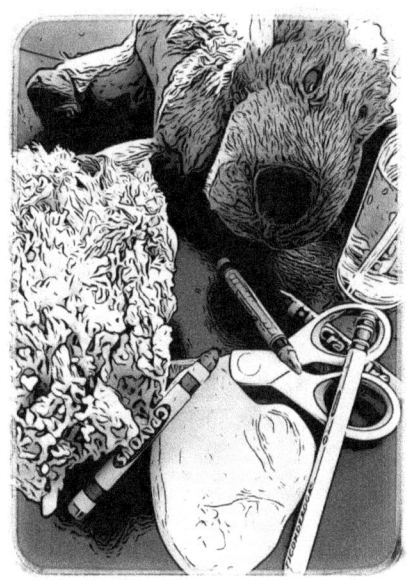

Have you ever been left completely in charge of twenty-five six-year-olds in a room filled with tiny scissors, sharp pencils, puppets, crayons, a snack cabinet, puzzles, a rocking chair, and a white board? What could go wrong?

Have you ever tried explaining to a mother how her daughter arrived at school with a ponytail and has a pixie cut at pick-up? To be fair, incidents like scalping are rare. And looking through a different lens reveals many joyful experiences swimming in a turbulent sea of tiny people and miniature chairs. The five years I spent as an aide in a kindergarten classroom fueled my personal growth in delicious ways.

A receptive adult can learn a lot from children.

The teacher I worked with was working on her doctorate. Squeezed for time and energy between her roles as teacher and student, Mrs. Warren needed backup, and I had the capability to step into the gap. It seems our pairing was written in the stars. She trusted my skills and often allowed me to teach beyond the scope of lunch and playground manners.

On a sunny spring day, I arrive in room 28 with supplies for a science lesson. I have a sponge, a pumice stone, paper, waxed paper, and a smooth stone. Today's science lesson is about absorption. After pouring water on every prop and observing the results, I ask the children to stand so that we can reinforce what we've witnessed for ourselves.

We explore the *sponge* as the children stand in a cluster with lots of space between them. I pull a few children from the group and ask them to demonstrate how they can freely pass through the openings between their friends. Next we investigate what happens when the group comes tightly together... We run into a *rock*.

Basic, yes? Yet I was witnessing minds in the acts of curiosity, learning, teaching, connecting, and creativity — minds including my own. The experience was magical — a feeling that makes living on this third rock from the sun a delight.

And I wonder...

What's possible when I make space to follow what's calling to me?

35

IN CONCERT

I'd say he's in his eighth decade — the bearded man two pews in front of me. His red and blue flannel plaid and a coordinating ruddy complexion paint pictures of farmland... or forest, in my mind's eye. There's something odd in the tilt of his wife's head, and the mechanics of her eyes and mouth seem unusual. I wonder if she's had a stroke or is surviving some peculiar disease, of which there are so many these days.

The pair has turned to the couple behind them for intermission conversation while the conductor, flutists, clarinetists, oboists, bassoonists, and horn and bass players catch their breath between arias and serenades.

I listen to the outdoorsman explain that he does not play music; he simply loves it. He and his wife have not come from their farm or cabin in the woods to the small town church... They've come from their home in the big city. *Ugh, me and my assumptions.*

Something about this man has touched something inside of me. I suspect it's because in my limited perceptions of who belongs where, he doesn't fit.

Do I think I fit? No, not really. I know next to nothing about classical music. When the event's availability popped up as an advertisement on my screen, something inside encouraged me to order the free ticket. And even though more than once I considered not coming, here I am.

During the second half of the performance, I watch his full head of gray-flecked, neatly-cut, blond hair bounce and weave in time above a warm-looking plaid collar as moderato flows into adagio and allegro into allegro energico. I watch my soul's observations and am a bit chagrined that they have very little to do with what I've come to witness.

When the conductor and musicians bow, the applause is long and loud from a crowd of less than one hundred hands. In the parking lot, I continue to key in on what has caught my interest. He escorts his wife to the passenger side of their vehicle and guides her into her seat with such gentleness that my heart sings. Once behind the wheel of my truck, I hear claps of appreciation vibrating at a frequency of my own choice.

And I wonder...

How often do we miss our heart's song because we're distracted by what's playing on the main stage?

ABOUT THE AUTHOR

Gail Boenning wanders, wonders, and writes.

She has learned that the stories we tell ourselves — and each other — shape our days and therefore, our lives.

ALSO BY GAIL BOENNING

www.ingramcontent.com/pod-product-compliance
Lightning Source LLC
Chambersburg PA
CBHW071233170626
46809CB00008BA/3043